READ, EXPLORE, AND DISCOVER

STEP IN

Fun learn-to-read stories and companion
activities to build confident readers!
PLUS flash cards and activities to practice the
words every young reader must know!

Senior Editor: Janet Sweet
Design/Production: Rebekah O. Lewis
Art Director: Moonhee Pak
Managing Editor: Stacey Faulkner

Table of Contents

Learn to READ Tips

Helping Your Child Learn to READ

Reading is the most important skill your child needs for success in school and in life. Helping your child learn to **read, explore, and discover** the world of written language today ensures a bright and successful future for your child tomorrow.

You Have Already Taken the First Step

From infancy through the preschool years, your child has already learned valuable **pre-reading** skills at home just by interacting with you as you talk, sing, recite nursery rhymes, and read aloud from stories, street signs, restaurant menus—even food labels. Activities like these built the necessary groundwork for your child to learn the sounds and names for letters and words, and to connect information with printed words. Now your child is ready to take the next step to becoming a reader!

The READ Series Helps You with the Next Step

Your child's success as a beginning reader requires the right stories and reading materials at the right time. Faced with so many beginning-to-read choices in the marketplace, it is often difficult for parents to know which ones are best for their children. The READ series by Creative Teaching Press has been specifically designed with your child's and your needs in mind. Engaging stories and expertly developed companion materials support a confident transition into successful early reading. Once children make the exhilarating discovery that they can read by themselves, their reading skills soar and there is simply no stopping them!

About the READ Series

Young children are naturally drawn to images and ideas that are all about their world. The **READ Stories** in each workbook feature amusing characters and visually appealing illustrations that engage your child's attention and nurture reading development. Each story is designed to encourage and support your child's reading efforts by providing:

- High-interest topics to beginning readers
- Humorous or surprise endings that encourage rereading
- Predictable story lines with repeating text
- Exposure to repeating sound and word patterns in familiar tales and rhymes

The stories in each workbook feature bright-colored art and whimsical illustrations in a broad mix of styles that naturally appeal to young children. At the bottom of every story page are **READ Picture Clue Prompts**. These are short, simple questions that encourage your beginning reader to use picture clues that are embedded in the illustrations to derive meaning from the story. This is an important skill in enabling children to deepen their reading enjoyment, language development, and comprehension.

In addition, each workbook features **Companion READ Activities** designed to reinforce and extend the skills introduced in each story, including:

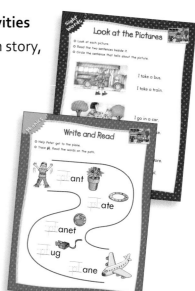

- Sight Words—to review the high-frequency words that your child must know by sight
- Phonics—to review letter sounds
- Vocabulary—to review new and unfamiliar words from each book
- Skill—to practice related learning skills from each book
- Activity—with easy directions to help your child create a collection of make-your-own mini-books related directly to the content and vocabulary of each story. Encourage your child to read the books often to build reading fluency.

Each RE**AD** workbook also features **Activities, Word Lists, and Flash Cards** to help your child practice recognizing the **Words Every Reader Must Know**. These are the most commonly used words in the English language, making up nearly 75% of everything a young child reads. Typically these "must-know" words do not follow regular spelling rules or phonics patterns, which makes them very difficult for beginning readers to recognize or sound out. The RE**AD** activities are designed to help your child develop mastery, confidence, and fluency when encountering these words in both reading and writing.

Parent Suggestions to Help Your Child READ

Here are some parent-friendly ideas for helping to make your child's learning-to-read experience relaxed, enjoyable, and stimulating:

- First, it is important to remember that children do not have to know all their letters and sounds before you put a story in their hands. Children are learning a great deal about reading at this point.

- Next, introduce each story by looking at and discussing the pictures <u>before</u> reading the story. This is called a *picture walk,* and it helps your child get a sense of what the story will be about. A preview such as this will help your child become familiar with and hear the sound of certain vocabulary words before they appear in print, as well as make predictions about the story's ending.

- Then, read the story aloud to your child. Feel free to read it aloud more than once. Most importantly, read aloud with enthusiasm and expression, which helps your child become familiar with the sentence patterns, vocabulary words, and story line. This will build your child's confidence in his or her attempts to read the story independently.

- Now read the story with your child. Actively involve your child as you read together by:
  - » Pointing to the words as you read.
  - » Guiding your child's finger or having him or her point to the words as you read.
  - » Reading a page and inviting your child to point and repeat after you.
  - » Reading the story together.
  - » Reading the story and pausing often so your child can supply the next word.
  - » Praising and encouraging your child's effort.

- Finally, read alongside your child. This is the exciting step when your child reads the story alone! It usually occurs spontaneously while you are sharing the story, and it is an exhilarating moment for your child.

- Don't worry if your child doesn't read each word perfectly the first time. There will be plenty of chances to develop accuracy as your child reads the story again and again. Encourage your child to tackle difficult words or phrases by:
  - » Looking at the related illustrations for clues and taking a guess.
  - » Reading beyond the difficult word for helpful clues from the next sentence.
  - » Replacing the difficult word or phrase by saying aloud "blank" and asking your child what would sound right or make sense.
  - » Rereading the sentence.
  - » Looking at the first letter for a clue to the initial sound.
  - » Sounding out the word.

Kids Like

1 Look at the picture. Name 2 things that children can do here.

2 What are the oranges and grapes sitting on?

R.E.A.D. Step In • Gr. PreK–K © 2010 Creative Teaching Press

We like to read.

1 Look behind the boy. Where do the children keep their books?

2 What are the children sitting on?

R.E.A.D. Step In • Gr. PreK–K © 2010 Creative Teaching Press

We like to write.

1 What does the girl like to write?

2 What does the boy like to write?

R.E.A.D. Step In • Gr. PreK–K © 2010 Creative Teaching Press

We like to draw.

1. Name 3 things the children are using to draw.

2. What is the boy drawing on the paper?

R.E.A.D. Step In • Gr. PreK–K © 2010 Creative Teaching Press

We like to paint.

1 What are the children using to paint with?

2 What is the brown thing that holds the picture of the flower?

R.E.A.D. Step In • Gr. PreK–K © 2010 Creative Teaching Press

We like to play.

1 What is the boy in the blue shirt holding?

2 Where are these children playing?

R.E.A.D. Step In • Gr. PreK–K © 2010 Creative Teaching Press

We like to build.

1 What are the children building with?

2 Who has the taller building?

R.E.A.D. Step In • Gr. PreK–K © 2010 Creative Teaching Press

We like lunch!

1 Where are the children eating?

2 Look at the children's lunches. What 2 things are the same for all of them?

R.E.A.D. Step In • Gr. PreK–K © 2010 Creative Teaching Press

What Is Missing?

Kids Like

☼ Look at the words in the Word Box.

☼ Read each sentence.

☼ Write the missing word.

Word Box

We	like	to

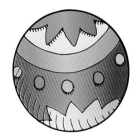

We _____ to play.

We like _____ read.

_____ like lunch!

Words That Rhyme

✪ Look at the words and pictures.

✪ Circle the picture that rhymes with the word.

read

like

book

write

R.E.A.D. Step In • Gr. PreK–K © 2010 Creative Teaching Press

Let's Play!

⚙ Look at the pictures.

⚙ Circle the pictures that go with a playground.

playground

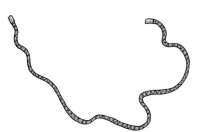

Picture Match

☼ Read the sentences.

☼ Look at the pictures.

☼ Draw a line from each sentence to its picture.

I build with blocks. •

I draw and color. •

I paint on paper. •

I eat my lunch. •

R.E.A.D. Step In • Gr. PreK–K © 2010 Creative Teaching Press

Make a Flip Book

☼ Cut along the <u>solid</u> lines.

☼ Staple the cards to the flip book.

☼ Read your book to tell what kids like to do.

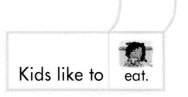

Kids like to   eat.

Kids like to

read.

write.

draw.

paint.

play.

build.

eat.

19

A Picnic

1 Why are these ants happy?

2 One ant's tongue is out. What does that mean?

R.E.A.D. Step In • Gr. PreK–K © 2010 Creative Teaching Press

We have a banana.

1 What are the ants doing with the banana?

2 What do you call the skin on a banana?

We have a carrot.

1 Why does the last ant look unhappy?

2 Why does the first ant look different from the last ant?

R.E.A.D. Step In • Gr. PreK–K © 2010 Creative Teaching Press

We have a pizza.

1 What is the shape of a full pizza?

2 What is the shape of the missing part of this pizza?

R.E.A.D. Step In • Gr. PreK–K © 2010 Creative Teaching Press

We have a hot dog.

1 Which ant is in charge? How do you know?

2 What are the little spots on the hot dog bun?

R.E.A.D. Step In • Gr. PreK–K © 2010 Creative Teaching Press

We have a pie.

1 The inside of the pie is purple. What kind of pie do you think it probably is?

2 What shape are the 3 holes on the top of the pie?

R.E.A.D. Step In • Gr. PreK–K © 2010 Creative Teaching Press

We have a cake.

① What is on the outside of the cake?

② Are the ants moving the pie to the right or to the left?

We have a picnic!
Yum! Yum!

1 Is it good that the ants have a lot of legs? Why?

2 What is the big purple thing behind the food?

R.E.A.D. Step In • Gr. PreK–K © 2010 Creative Teaching Press

A Picnic

What Is Missing?

☺ Look at the words in the Word Box.

☺ Read each sentence.

☺ Write the missing word.

Word Box

We   have   a

We have _____ pizza.

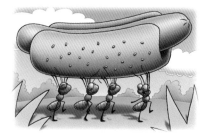
We _____ a hot dog.

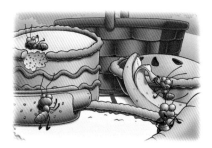
_____ have a picnic!

Find the Pie

A Picnic

✿ Help the ants find the pie.

✿ Say the name of each picture on the path.

✿ Circle the pictures that begin with **p**.

R.E.A.D. Step In • Gr. PreK–K © 2010 Creative Teaching Press

What Goes With a Picnic?

⚙ Look at the pictures.

⚙ Circle the pictures that go with a picnic.

picnic

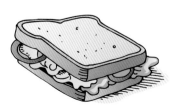

In the Right Order

A Picnic

☼ Look at the pictures.

☼ Write 1, 2, 3, and 4 in the circles to show the story order.

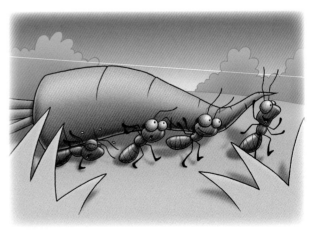

R.E.A.D. Step In • Gr. PreK–K © 2010 Creative Teaching Press

Make a Flip Book

⚙ Cut along the <u>solid</u> lines.

⚙ Staple the cards to the flip book.

⚙ Read about what you will eat.

I will eat 4 carrots

I will eat

1 banana.

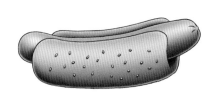

2 hot dogs.

3 cookies.

4 carrots.

5 cherries.

6 grapes.

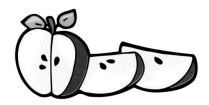

7 apples.

R.E.A.D. Step In • Gr. PreK–K © 2010 Creative Teaching Press

I Like Colors

1 Does Cat like paint? How do you know?

2 What is Dog looking at? Why?

R.E.A.D. Step In • Gr. PreK–K © 2010 Creative Teaching Press

I like **red.**

1 Is Dog a careful painter? How do you know?

2 What kind of bug is on the window?

R.E.A.D. Step In • Gr. PreK–K © 2010 Creative Teaching Press

I like **blue.**

1 Look at Dog's paintbrush and Cat's paintbrush. How are they different?

2 How does Cat paint differently than Dog?

R.E.A.D. Step In • Gr. PreK–K © 2010 Creative Teaching Press

I like yellow.

1 What is Dog painting yellow?

2 What is Dog standing on?

R.E.A.D. Step In • Gr. PreK–K © 2010 Creative Teaching Press

I like **purple.**

1 What is Dog painting purple?

2 What shape is on Dog's eye and on the flowers?

R.E.A.D. Step In • Gr. PreK–K © 2010 Creative Teaching Press

I like green.

1 What 3 paint colors are on Cat's hat?

2 Cat's tongue is out. What do you think that means?

R.E.A.D. Step In • Gr. PreK–K © 2010 Creative Teaching Press

I like orange.

1 What is Cat painting orange?

2 Name 2 more things that are orange in this picture.

R.E.A.D. Step In • Gr. PreK–K © 2010 Creative Teaching Press

I like colors!

1 Name all the paint colors that Cat and Dog used.

2 What is another word for a clubhouse?

R.E.A.D. Step In • Gr. PreK–K © 2010 Creative Teaching Press

I Like Colors

Color Words

☼ Look at the words and pictures.
☼ Draw a line to match each color word to its picture.

· yellow ·

· red ·

· green ·

· blue ·

R.E.A.D. Step In • Gr. PreK–K © 2010 Creative Teaching Press

Words that Rhyme

- Look at the words and pictures.
- Circle the picture that rhymes with the word.

I		
can		
red		
like		

R.E.A.D. Step In • Gr. PreK–K © 2010 Creative Teaching Press

Let's Write and Paint!

Vocabulary

⚙ Look at the words and pictures.

⚙ Draw a line from each word to its matching pictures.

· write ·

· paint ·

Yellow

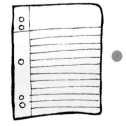

BLUE

Picture Match

⚙ Look at the pictures.

⚙ Circle the word that matches each picture.

   cat   cats

   can   cans

   house   houses

   car   cars

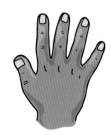   hand   hands

R.E.A.D. Step In • Gr. PreK–K © 2010 Creative Teaching Press

Make a Mini Book

✪ Write your name on the first page.

✪ Cut along the <u>solid</u> lines.

✪ Fold along the <u>dotted</u> lines and staple.

✪ Name the missing color word on each page.

Color Rhymes

by

_____

What color rhymes with **fellow**?

4

What color rhymes with **seen**?

5

What color rhymes with **town**?

8

Color Rhymes

by

_____

1

Make a Mini Book

What color rhymes with **sack**?

6

What color rhymes with **glue**?

3

What color rhymes with **bed**?

2

What color rhymes with **sink**?

7

48

On the Go

1 Look at the picture. Name 3 things that can help you go somewhere.

2 Is the girl going safely? How do you know?

R.E.A.D. Step In • Gr. PreK–K © 2010 Creative Teaching Press

A bus takes me to school.

1 Name 2 things the girl has for school.

2 Why is there a stop sign on the bus?

R.E.A.D. Step In • Gr. PreK–K © 2010 Creative Teaching Press

A car takes me to the market.

1 How did this family get to the market?

2 The sign says "SPECIAL CARROTS."
What does that mean?

R.E.A.D. Step In • Gr. PreK–K © 2010 Creative Teaching Press

A bike takes me to the park.

1 Does the girl drive the bike or ride the bike?

2 What is the difference?

R.E.A.D. Step In • Gr. PreK–K © 2010 Creative Teaching Press

A train takes me to the city.

1 Look at the picture. Is the train in the city yet? How do you know?

2 What is the man reading?

R.E.A.D. Step In • Gr. PreK–K © 2010 Creative Teaching Press

A plane takes me to Grandpa's.

1 Look at the picture. Who is "me"?

2 Is the boy happy to see Grandpa? How do you know?

R.E.A.D. Step In • Gr. PreK–K © 2010 Creative Teaching Press

But my feet take me . . .

1 What is this ☆ shape?

2 How many ☆ are there in this picture?

R.E.A.D. Step In • Gr. PreK–K © 2010 Creative Teaching Press

to the ice-cream store!

1 Look at the sign. Now look at the boy's ice-cream cone. How are they the same?

2 How are they different?

R.E.A.D. Step In • Gr. PreK–K © 2010 Creative Teaching Press

Look at the Pictures

- ✿ Look at each picture.
- ✿ Read the two sentences beside it.
- ✿ Circle the sentence that tells about the picture.

I take a bus.

I take a train.

I go in a car.

I go on a bike.

I go to the store.

I go to school.

Write and Read

☼ Help Peter get to the plane.

☼ Trace **pl**. Read the words on the path.

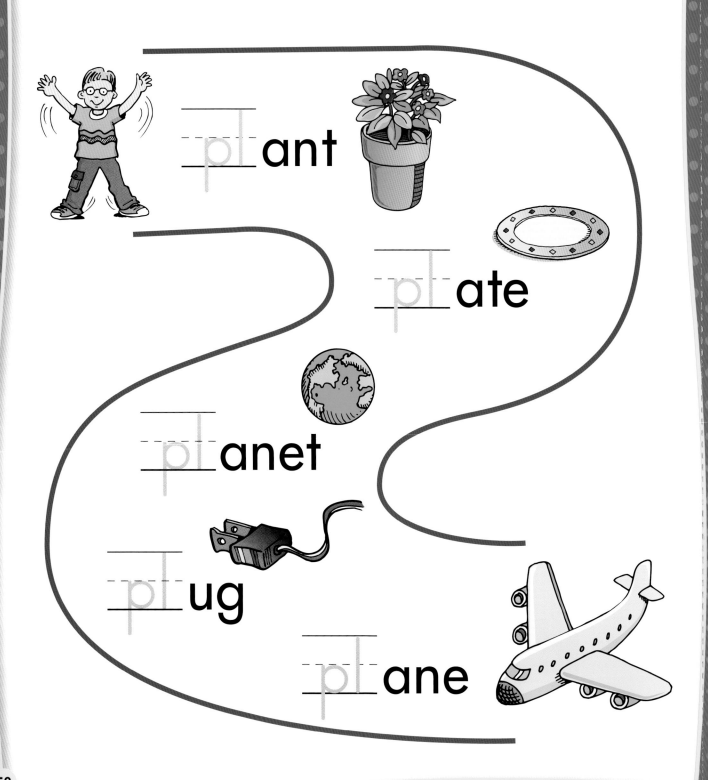

plant

plate

planet

plug

plane

R.E.A.D. Step In • Gr. PreK–K © 2010 Creative Teaching Press

Going to Grandma's

- Jill will go to Grandma's house.
- Circle what will take her there.
- Trace the paths to find out.

bike

bus

car

store

Grandma's house

park

Where Do They Go?

☼ Look at the pictures on the sides of the page.

☼ Draw a line to show where each one goes.

car •

• helicopter

in the air

plane •

on land

• sailboat

in the water

ship •

• train

R.E.A.D. Step In • Gr. PreK–K © 2010 Creative Teaching Press

On the Go Flip Book

⚙ Cut along the <u>solid</u> lines.

⚙ Staple the cards to the flip book.

⚙ Read your book.

Here is a 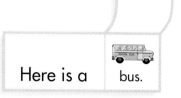 bus.

Here is a  car.

bus.

bike.

train.

plane.

van.

ship.

R.E.A.D. Step In • Gr. PreK–K © 2010 Creative Teaching Press

Here Is My Cat

1 How are the cats the same?

2 How are the cats different?

R.E.A.D. Step In • Gr. PreK–K © 2010 Creative Teaching Press

Here is my cat.

1 Is the girl at home or at school?
How do you know?

2 Find the ♪. What does that mean?

R.E.A.D. Step In • Gr. PreK–K © 2010 Creative Teaching Press

My cat is in the tree.

1 Look at the girl and the cat. What do they have on that is the same?

2 What part of the tree is the cat on?

65

Here is my cat.

1 Does the cat like the boy? How do you know?

2 How is the boy's hair the same as the cat's fur?

R.E.A.D. Step In • Gr. PreK–K © 2010 Creative Teaching Press

My cat is in the box.

1 What is on the cat's head?

2 Find the mouse. What is it doing?

R.E.A.D. Step In • Gr. PreK–K © 2010 Creative Teaching Press

Here is my cat.
My cat is in the bag.

1 What kind of bag is the cat in?

2 What kind of store did the girl go to? How do you know?

R.E.A.D. Step In • Gr. PreK–K © 2010 Creative Teaching Press

Here is my cat.

1 What kind of cat is this?

2 How is this cat the same as the cats on page 63?

R.E.A.D. Step In • Gr. PreK–K © 2010 Creative Teaching Press

My cat is in the zoo!

1 How is this cat different from the cats on page 63?

2 What other animals do you see here?

R.E.A.D. Step In • Gr. PreK–K © 2010 Creative Teaching Press

Draw and Read

Here Is My Cat

⚙ Draw a line under **is**.

⚙ Draw a circle around **the**.

My cat is in the tree.

My cat is in the box.

My cat is in the bag.

My cat is in the zoo.

R.E.A.D. Step In • Gr. PreK–K © 2010 Creative Teaching Press

Find the Cat

Here Is My Cat

⊛ Help Dan find the cat.

⊛ Say the name of each picture on the path.

⊛ Circle the pictures that begin with **c**.

R.E.A.D. Step In • Gr. PreK–K © 2010 Creative Teaching Press

Zoo or House?

- Look at the words and pictures.
- Draw a line from each word to its matching pictures.

ZOO

house

In the Right Order

⚙ Look at the pictures.

⚙ Write 1, 2, 3, and 4 in the circles to show the story order.

Make a Mini Book

- Write your name on the first page.
- Cut along the <u>solid</u> lines and staple.
- Read your book about cats.

Cats, Cats!
by

_____

- - - - - - - - - - -

_____

1

There are yellow cats.

2

There are brown cats.

3

There are orange cats.

4

There are small cats.

5

And there are BIG cats!

6

I Can See

1 What are the little pink mice carrying?

2 Look at the title of the story. Why is this picture funny?

R.E.A.D. Step In • Gr. PreK–K © 2010 Creative Teaching Press

I can see the cat.

1 What is the purple thing that the mouse is standing on?

2 Are the mice afraid of this cat? How do you know?

R.E.A.D. Step In • Gr. PreK–K © 2010 Creative Teaching Press

It is on the mat.
It has a funny hat.

1 Look at the cat and the hat. Name 2 shapes that you see.

2 Would a real cat and mouse wear clothes? Why?

R.E.A.D. Step In • Gr. PreK–K © 2010 Creative Teaching Press

I can see the frog.

1 Look at both of these pages. What are the yellow animals by the log?

2 How many are there?

R.E.A.D. Step In • Gr. PreK–K © 2010 Creative Teaching Press

It is on the log.
It has a little dog.

1 What is the frog holding in its hand? Why?

2 What 3 words rhyme on these pages?

R.E.A.D. Step In • Gr. PreK–K © 2010 Creative Teaching Press

I can see the bug.

1 Look at what is on the bug's back. Is it to drink or to eat? How do you know?

2 Look at both of these pages. What is in the middle of the rug?

R.E.A.D. Step In • Gr. PreK–K © 2010 Creative Teaching Press

It is on the rug.
It has a big mug.

1 What are the worms wearing?

2 What kinds of food are they carrying?

R.E.A.D. Step In • Gr. PreK–K © 2010 Creative Teaching Press

I can see the bee.
It is in the tree.
Now it is on me!

1 What is the red animal on the tree?

2 What 4 words rhyme on this page?

R.E.A.D. Step In • Gr. PreK–K © 2010 Creative Teaching Press

What Can You See?

I Can See

- Look at the words in the Word Box.
- Read each sentence.
- Write the missing word.

Word Box

| I | can | see |

I can _____ the cat.

I _____ see the frog.

_____ can see the bee.

Write and Rhyme

I Can See

☼ Trace the letters in each set of rhyming words.

frog

dog

bee

tree

bug

rug

R.E.A.D. Step In • Gr. PreK–K © 2010 Creative Teaching Press

In the Tree

⚙ Read the words. Then write the words in the right boxes.

⚙ Write a sentence about the picture on the lines below.

Word Box

| tree | bird | ant | boy | bee |

_____

_____

_____

R.E.A.D. Step In • Gr. PreK–K © 2010 Creative Teaching Press

What Goes Together?

I Can See

☼ Cross out one thing in each row that does not belong.

☼ Then draw something that does go with the other things.

R.E.A.D. Step In • Gr. PreK–K © 2010 Creative Teaching Press

Make a Flip Book

- Cut along the <u>solid</u> lines.
- Staple the cards to the flip book.
- Read about what you can see.

I see a

I see a dog.

cat.

hat.

bug.

mug.

frog.

log.

89

First 100 Words Every Reader Must Know

a	did	if	on	this
about	do	in	one	three
after	down	is	or	to
again	eat	it	other	two
all	for	just	our	up
an	from	know	out	us
and	get	like	put	very
any	give	little	said	was
are	go	long	see	we
as	good	make	she	were
at	had	man	so	what
be	has	many	some	when
been	have	me	take	which
before	he	much	that	who
boy	her	my	the	will
but	here	new	their	with
by	him	no	them	work
can	his	not	then	would
come	how	of	there	you
day	I	old	they	your

R.E.A.D. Step In • Gr. PreK–K © 2010 Creative Teaching Press

Second 100 Words Every Reader Must Know

also	each	left	own	sure
am	ear	let	people	tell
another	end	live	play	than
away	far	look	please	these
back	find	made	present	thing
ball	first	may	pretty	think
because	five	men	ran	too
best	found	more	read	tree
better	four	morning	red	under
big	friend	most	right	until
black	girl	mother	run	upon
book	got	must	saw	use
both	hand	name	say	want
box	high	near	school	way
bring	home	never	seem	where
call	house	next	shall	while
came	into	night	should	white
color	kind	only	soon	why
could	last	open	stand	wish
dear	leave	over	such	year

R.E.A.D. Step In • Gr. PreK–K © 2010 Creative Teaching Press

Third 100 Words Every Reader Must Know

along	don't	grow	off	stop
always	door	happy	once	ten
anything	dress	hard	order	thank
around	early	hat	pair	third
ask	eight	head	part	those
ate	every	hear	ride	though
bed	eyes	help	round	today
brown	face	hold	same	took
buy	fall	hope	sat	town
car	fast	hot	second	try
carry	fat	jump	set	turn
clean	fine	keep	seven	walk
close	fire	letter	show	warm
clothes	fly	longer	sing	wash
coat	food	love	sister	water
cold	full	might	sit	woman
cut	funny	money	six	write
didn't	gave	myself	sleep	yellow
does	goes	now	small	yes
dog	green	o'clock	start	yesterday

R.E.A.D. Step In • Gr. PreK–K © 2010 Creative Teaching Press

Words Every Reader Must Know
in each **READ** Story

Kids Like

like	to	write
we	read	play

A Picnic

a	have	dog
we	hot	

I Like Colors

I	color(s)	blue	green
like	red	yellow	

On the Go

on	a	to	but
the	take(s)	school	my
go	me	car	

Here Is My Cat

here	my	the	box
is	in	tree	

I Can See

I	it	funny	big	me
can	is	hat	in	
see	on	little	tree	
the	has	dog	now	

R.E.A.D. Step In • Gr. PreK–K © 2010 Creative Teaching Press

Sentence Skills

Words Every Reader Must Know

⚙ Look at the words in the word box.

⚙ Write the missing word in each sentence.

Word Box

play	and	can
the	go	good

1 I want to _____.

2 We see _____ cat.

3 The car can _____.

Sentence Skills

Words Every Reader Must Know

⚙ Look at the words in the word box.

⚙ Write the missing word in each sentence.

Word Box

if	is	for
were	was	we

1 He _____ not little.

2 It is _____ you.

3 When can _____ go?

R.E.A.D. Step In • Gr. PreK–K © 2010 Creative Teaching Press

Sentence Skills

○ Look at the words in the word box.

○ Write the missing word in each sentence.

Word Box

they	that	much
make	at	eat

1 I will take _____.

2 They like us very _____.

3 We like to _____.

R.E.A.D. Step In • Gr. PreK–K © 2010 Creative Teaching Press

Mini-Book Activity

Words Every Reader Must Know

Follow the easy directions below to make your own mini-book.

 **Directions**

1. Tear out pages 99-102.

2. Cut the pages apart along the solid line.

3. Staple them together.

4. Write your name on the author line. You can also write the name of a special person on the dedication line.

5. Next, write the missing word on each page of the mini-book.
   (Hint: Most of the missing words are repeated in the mini-book story.)

6. Then use crayons, colored pencils, or markers to color the pages.

7. Practice reading the mini-book story aloud. Now you are ready to share your mini-book with your family and friends!

R.E.A.D. Step In • Gr. PreK–K © 2010 Creative Teaching Press

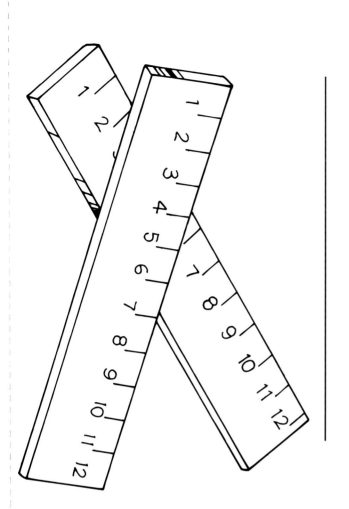

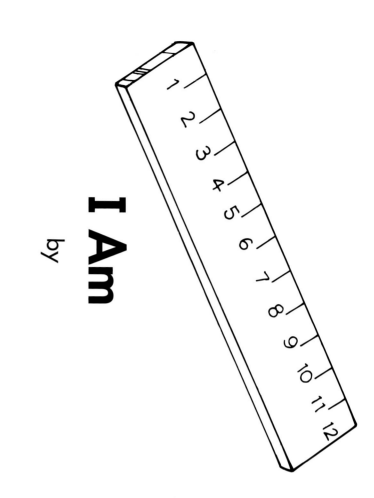

I Am

by

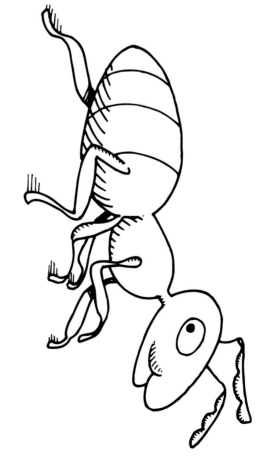

I am as small

as _____ ant.

1

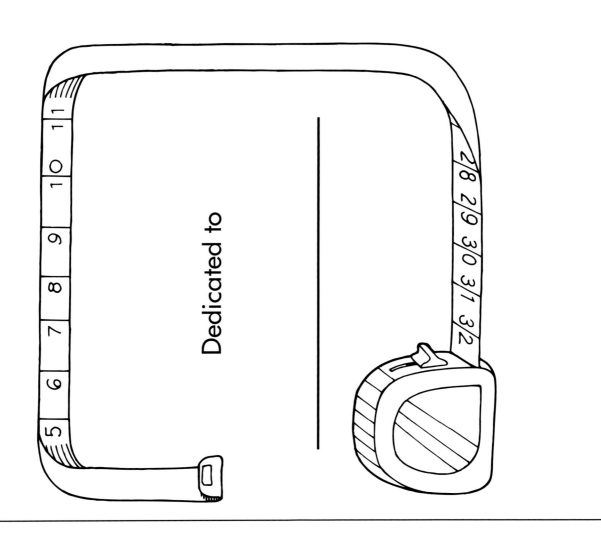

Dedicated to

_____

I am as big

an elephant. _____

2

busy as a bee.

_____ am as

5

small as a snail.

I _____ as

3

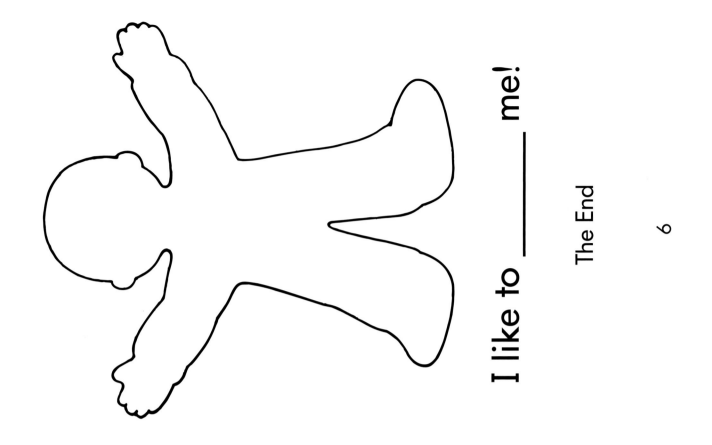

I like to _____ me!

The End

6

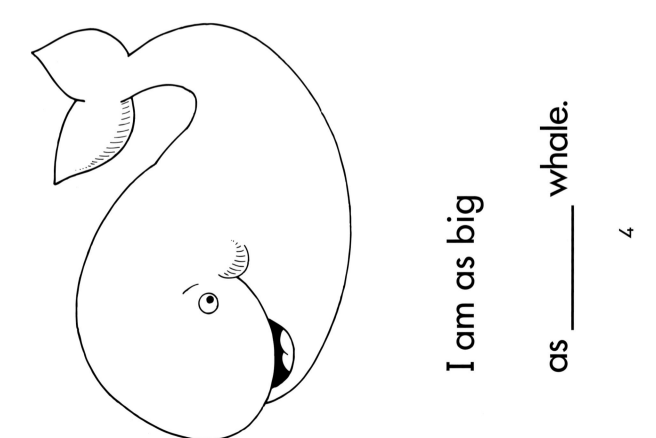

I am as big

as _____ whale.

4

102

Flash Card Game Ideas

Words Every Reader Must Know

Flash cards for the First 100 Words Every Reader Must Know appear on the following pages to support beginning readers in Pre-Kindergarten and Kindergarten. Here are some game ideas for using the flash cards.

Play a sorting game

- Sort the flash cards into alphabetical order.
- Sort the flash cards by words that begin with the same letter.
- Sort the flash cards by words that rhyme. Think of additional words that rhyme and say them aloud or write them down.

Play a memory game

- Before cutting apart the flash cards, make a photocopy of each page to create a set of one-sided cards. Create a set of game cards by pulling out just one pair of cards for each beginning letter found in the flash cards. Turn these cards facedown to play a memory game. Each player takes a turn by turning over two cards at a time to read aloud the pair of words. If both words begin with the same letter, then that player gets to keep the pair of cards and take another turn. If the words do not begin with the same letter, then the next player gets to take a turn. The game continues until all the pairs of cards have been correctly paired.
- As a variation of this game, players must read aloud the pair of words and use each word in a sentence.

Other activities

- Use a timer to see how quickly each word can be read aloud. Begin with a small number of cards at first. Then add more cards as speed and confidence increases.
- Brainstorm another word that begins with the same sound as each flash card word.
- Use the blank flash cards to add other words to the flash card set.

R.E.A.D. Step In • Gr. PreK–K © 2010 Creative Teaching Press

a	about
after	again
all	an
and	any
are	as

R.E.A.D. Step In • Gr. PreK–K © 2010 Creative Teaching Press

at	be
been	before
boy	but
by	can
come	day

did	do
down	eat
for	from
get	give
go	good

R.E.A.D. Step In • Gr. PreK–K © 2010 Creative Teaching Press

had	has
have	he
her	here
him	his
how	I

if	in
is	it
just	know
like	little
long	make

R.E.A.D. Step In • Gr. PreK–K © 2010 Creative Teaching Press

man	many
me	much
my	new
no	not
of	old

on	one
or	other
our	out
put	said
see	she

R.E.A.D. Step In • Gr. PreK–K © 2010 Creative Teaching Press

so	some
take	that
the	their
them	then
there	they

R.E.A.D. Step In • Gr. PreK–K © 2010 Creative Teaching Press

this	three
to	two
up	us
very	was
we	were

what	when
which	who
will	with
work	would
you	your

R.E.A.D. Step In • Gr. PreK–K © 2010 Creative Teaching Press

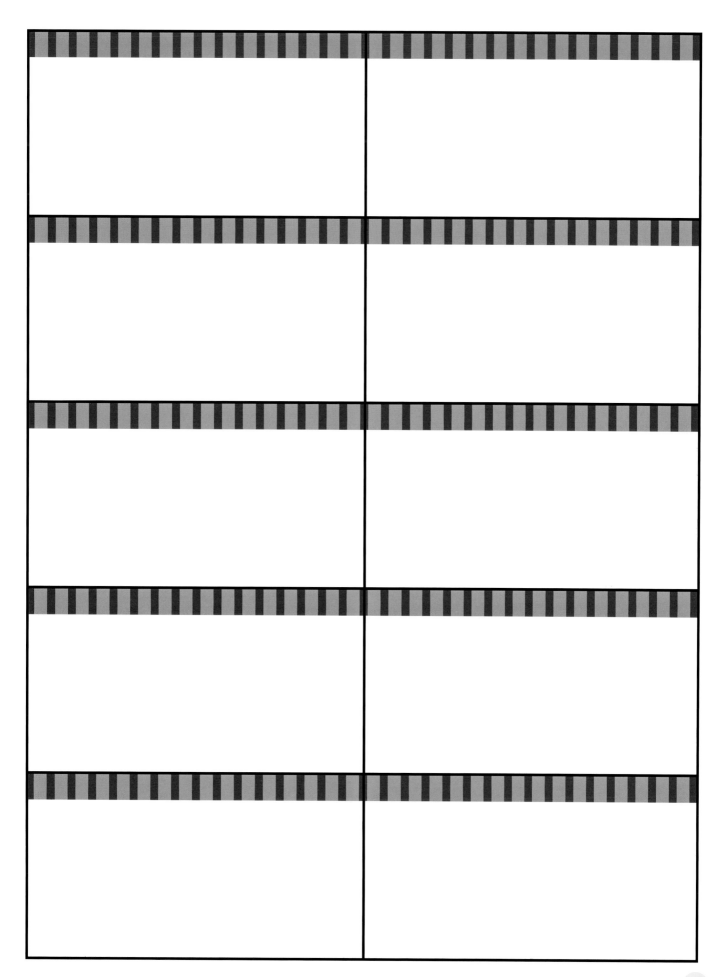

Answer Key READ Story Questions

Kids Like

PAGE 7
- Color; draw; read; play; eat
- A napkin

PAGE 8
- On a bookshelf
- Possible answers: Beanbag chairs; cushions

PAGE 9
- *cat*
- *dog*

PAGE 10
- Crayons; markers; chalk
- A boat

PAGE 11
- A paintbrush and their hands
- An easel

PAGE 12
- A jump rope
- Possible answers: At a playground; at a park; at recess

PAGE 13
- Blocks
- The boy

PAGE 14
- Possible answers: At a table; at school; in the lunchroom
- Milk and a sandwich

A Picnic

PAGE 21
- Because they see a picnic and want to eat the food
- The ant is hungry.

PAGE 22
- Carrying the banana away
- The peel

PAGE 23
- The last ant is carrying the most weight.
- Possible answers: The first ant is happy; it does not have much to carry.

PAGE 24
- A circle
- A triangle

PAGE 25
- The first ant—because it is pointing and giving directions to the other ants
- Seeds

Answer Key READ Story Questions

PAGE 26
- Blueberry; blackberry
- Triangle

PAGE 27
- Icing; frosting
- To the right

PAGE 28
- Yes—because they can hold and eat more food with them
- A picnic basket

I Like Colors

PAGE 35
- Yes—because there is a heart in a thought bubble over Cat's head
- At the paint drips—because they might spill on Dog

PAGE 36
- Yes—because Dog does not spill or drip the paint
- A ladybug

PAGE 37
- Dog's is small and Cat's is big.
- Cat paints sloppier than Dog.

PAGE 38
- A roof
- A ladder

PAGE 39
- A window; a flowerbox
- A circle (spot)

PAGE 40
- Orange, blue, green
- That Cat is working very hard; that Cat is concentrating

PAGE 41
- A door
- Cat; the paint; the paintbrush; the flower

PAGE 42
- Red; blue; yellow; purple; green; orange
- Possible answers: Playhouse; fort

On the Go

PAGE 49
- Airplane; bus; car; roller blades
- Possible answers: Yes—because she is wearing knee and wrist pads; no — because she is not wearing a helmet

Answer Key READ Story Questions

PAGE 50

- A backpack; a lunch bag
- Possible answer: To stop traffic when children get on and off the bus

PAGE 51

- By car
- The carrots are on sale.

PAGE 52

- Ride
- Possible answer: You drive a car.

PAGE 53

- Yes—because there are tall buildings
- A newspaper

PAGE 54

- The boy
- Yes—because he is running to him

PAGE 55

- A star
- 11

PAGE 56

- Both have 2 scoops; both have a pink scoop on top of a brown scoop
- The sign has a cherry with brown sprinkles on the pink scoop and white sprinkles on the brown scoop, but the boy's cone does not.

Here Is My Cat

PAGE 63

- They have similar features. Possible answers: 4 legs; whiskers; a furry body; a tail; paws
- They have different fur colors; different nose colors; different patterns of fur— solid, spots

PAGE 64

- At home—because that is a house behind her
- That the bird is singing

PAGE 65

- Bows
- A tree branch

PAGE 66

- Yes—the cat is brushing its face against the boy.
- Both are orange.

PAGE 67

- A bow; ribbons
- Laughing

PAGE 68

- A paper bag; a grocery bag
- A grocery store—because there are bags of food

Answer Key READ Story Questions

PAGE 69

- A tiger
- It has similar features. Possible answers: 4 legs; whiskers; a furry body; a tail; paws

PAGE 70

- Possible answers: It is bigger; it is a wild animal; it lives in a zoo.
- A giraffe; an alligator; a lion; a butterfly

I Can See

PAGE 77

- A hat
- The mice can't see where they are going.

PAGE 78

- A ladder
- No—they are smiling.

PAGE 79

- Stripes (or lines), dots (or circles), triangles
- Possible answers: No—because they don't need them; maybe—as a costume

PAGE 80

- Ducks
- 4

PAGE 81

- A leash (or string, rope)—so the dog will not run away
- *frog, log, dog*

PAGE 82

- To drink—it has a straw
- Flowers; a flower vase

PAGE 83

- Sunglasses; a cap
- A cupcake and a hamburger

PAGE 84

- A raccoon; a squirrel
- *see, bee, tree, me*

Answer Key **READ** Story Companion Activities

What Is Missing?

- Look at the words in the Word Box.
- Read each sentence.
- Write the missing word.

Word Box

We	like	to

We _like_ to play.

We like _to_ read.

_We_ like lunch!

15

Words That Rhyme

- Look at the words and pictures.
- Circle the picture that rhymes with the word.

read

like

book

write

16

Let's Play!

- Look at the pictures.
- Circle the pictures that go with a playground.

playground

17

Picture Match

- Read the sentences.
- Look at the pictures.
- Draw a line from each sentence to its picture.

I build with blocks.

I draw and color.

I paint on paper.

I eat my lunch.

18

Answer Key READ Story Companion Activities

Sight Words

What Is Missing?

☺ Look at the words in the Word Box.
☺ Read each sentence.
☺ Write the missing word.

Word Box

We	have	a

We have __a__ pizza.

We __have__ a hot dog.

__We__ have a picnic!

29

Find the Pie

☺ Help the ants find the pie.
☺ Say the name of each picture on the path.
☺ Circle the pictures that begin with **p**.

30

What Goes With a Picnic?

☺ Look at the pictures.
☺ Circle the pictures that go with a picnic.

picnic

31

In the Right Order

☺ Look at the pictures.
☺ Write 1, 2, 3, and 4 in the circles to show the story order.

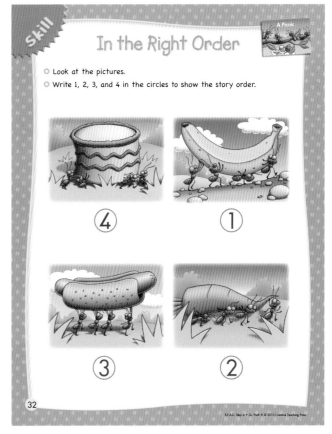

④   ①

③   ②

32

121

Answer Key R[E]AD Story Companion Activities

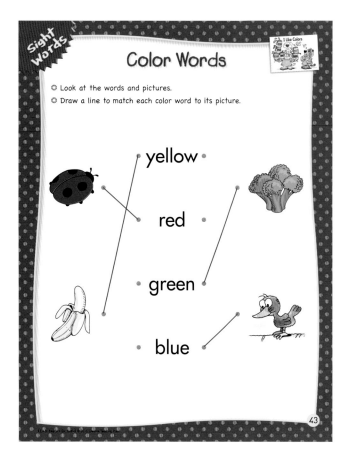

Color Words

⚙ Look at the words and pictures.
⚙ Draw a line to match each color word to its picture.

43

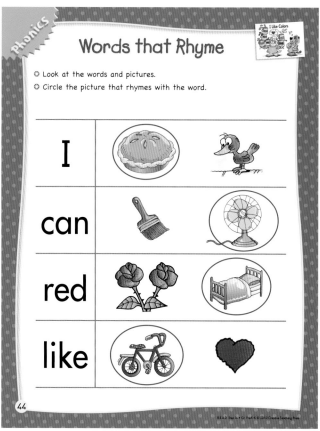

Words that Rhyme

⚙ Look at the words and pictures.
⚙ Circle the picture that rhymes with the word.

44

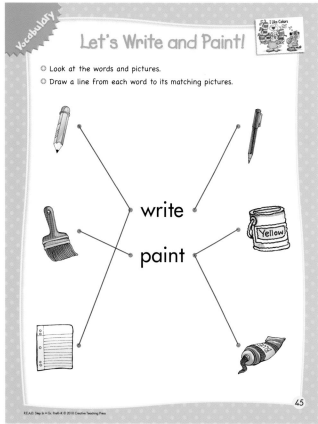

Let's Write and Paint!

⚙ Look at the words and pictures.
⚙ Draw a line from each word to its matching pictures.

45

Picture Match

⚙ Look at the pictures.
⚙ Circle the word that matches each picture.

46

Answer Key READ Story Companion Activities

Look at the Pictures

- Look at each picture.
- Read the two sentences beside it.
- Circle the sentence that tells about the picture.

(I take a bus.)

I take a train.

I go in a car.

(I go on a bike.)

(I go to the store.)

I go to school.

57

Write and Read

- Help Peter get to the plane.
- Trace **pl**. Read the words on the path.

plant

plate

planet

plug

plane

58

Going to Grandma's

- Jill will go to Grandma's house.
- Circle what will take her there.
- Trace the paths to find out.

bike   bus   car

store   Grandma's house   park

59

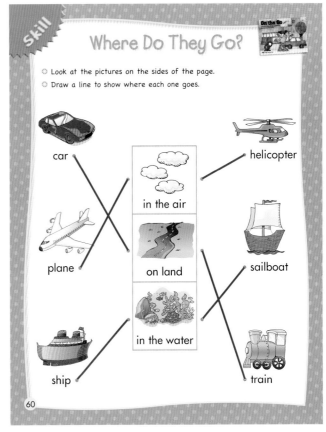

Where Do They Go?

- Look at the pictures on the sides of the page.
- Draw a line to show where each one goes.

car   helicopter

in the air

plane   sailboat

on land

in the water

ship   train

60

Answer Key READ Story Companion Activities

Here Is My Cat

Sight Words

Draw and Read

◌ Draw a line under **is**.
◌ Draw a circle around **the**.

My cat <u>is</u> in (the) tree.

My cat <u>is</u> in (the) box.

My cat <u>is</u> in (the) bag.

My cat <u>is</u> in (the) zoo.

71

Phonics

Find the Cat

◌ Help Dan find the cat.
◌ Say the name of each picture on the path.
◌ Circle the pictures that begin with **c**.

72

Vocabulary

Zoo or House?

◌ Look at the words and pictures.
◌ Draw a line from each word to its matching pictures.

zoo

house

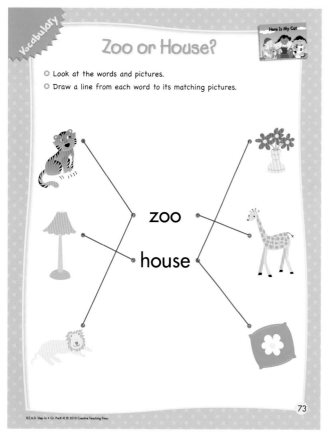

73

Skill

In the Right Order

◌ Look at the pictures.
◌ Write 1, 2, 3, and 4 in the circles to show the story order.

③   ①

④   ②

74

Answer Key READ Story Companion Activities

Sight Words

What Can You See?

- Look at the words in the Word Box.
- Read each sentence.
- Write the missing word.

Word Box

I	can	see

I can __see__ the cat.

I __can__ see the frog.

__I__ can see the bee.

85

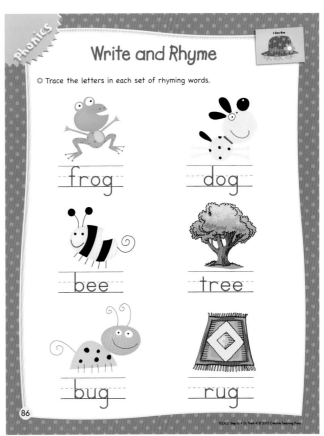

Phonics

Write and Rhyme

- Trace the letters in each set of rhyming words.

frog   dog

bee   tree

bug   rug

86

Vocabulary

In the Tree

- Read the words. Then write the words in the right boxes.
- Write a sentence about the picture on the lines below.

Word Box

tree	bird	ant	boy	bee

bird   ant
boy   bee
tree

Answers will vary.

87

Skill

What Goes Together?

- Cross out one thing in each row that does not belong.
- Then draw something that does go with the other things.

Picture will vary.

Picture will vary.

Picture will vary.

88

125

Answer Key
Sentence Skills
Words Every Reader Must Know

PAGE 95:

1. I want to **play**.
2. We see **the** cat.
3. The car can **go**.

PAGE 96:

1. He **is** not little.
2. It is **for** you.
3. When can **we** go?

PAGE 97:

1. I will take **that**.
2. They like us very **much**.
3. We like to **eat**.

Mini-Book
Words Every Reader Must Know

PAGE 99

- I am as small as **an** ant.

PAGE 100:

- I am as big **as** an elephant.

PAGE 101

- **I** am as busy as a bee.
- I **am** as small as a snail.

PAGE 102:

- I am as big as **a** whale. I like to **be** me!

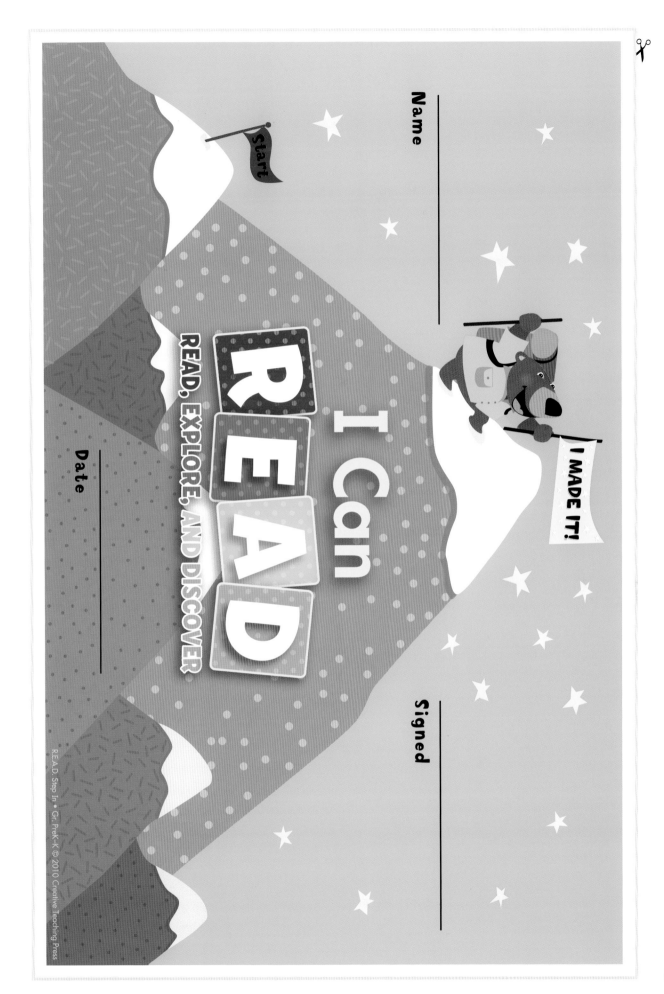

Name

Date

Signed

I Can READ

READ, EXPLORE, AND DISCOVER

Start

I MADE IT!

R.E.A.D. Step In • Gr. PreK-K © 2010 Creative Teaching Press

127